believe
you
can

DATE:___/___/___

Thoughts have energy and when you read these quotes that energy surrounds you and influence your subconscious mind in a positive way. Work with these quotes everyday by reading them and by writing your thoughts and ideas in your inspirational journal – notebook – diary.

Remember to always transform these words and quotes into positive actions to start seeing the results you want. Inspirational quotes are thoughts put into words, you just need to add action and all your thoughts will become a reality. If You Believe it, You Can do It!

These inspirational quotes included in your motivational journal will boost your confidence and will remind you to take action. Once you read them every day, they will change your state of mind and you will start to feel more positive.

Every time you write on your journal – notebook – diary you will be reminded to move forward with a great positive and inspirational quote. Use these quotes as a part of your daily habits and routines by reading them and don't forget to write down your own thoughts and ideas in your new inspirational journal – notebook – diary.

"The best way to gain self-confidence is to do what you are afraid to do." – Unknown

DATE:___/___/___

MAKE IT HAPPEN

Remember to be consistent, be persistent and always be positive. These quotes will set your mind for success and achievement while you write down all your ideas and thoughts. You can share these quotes with your family and loved ones and gather to write down more great ideas and positive thoughts together. This beautiful inspirational journal – notebook – diary will bring you the support you need to move forward with a positive thinking mind. Let this journal be the tool for your daily inspiration.

To your success!

DATE:___/___/___

"Believe in miracles but above all believe in yourself!"

DATE:___/___/___

BELIEVE IN YOURSELF

*"Never be afraid to start something new,
if you fail it is just temporary, if you believe and
persist you will succeed"*

DATE:___/___/___

TAKE ACTION!

"Wherever you go, go with all your heart." - Confucius

DATE:___/___/___

"Build your own dreams or you will end up
building someone else's dreams"

never give up

"*Your dreams and your goals are the seeds
of your own success*"

DATE:___/___/___

"Never give up, keep going no matter what!"

MAKE IT
HAPPEN

DATE:___/___/___

"Start where you are and take chances"

DATE:___/___/___

believe you can

think
POSITIVE

"Life isn't about finding yourself.
Life is about creating yourself." - George Bernard Shaw

DATE:____/____/____

BELIEVE IN YOURSELF

DATE:___/___/___

think positive

"CHANGE YOUR LIFE TODAY. DON'T GAMBLE ON THE FUTURE, ACT NOW, WITHOUT DELAY." — SIMONE DE BEAUVOIR

DATE:____/____/____

"The person who says it cannot be done should not interrupt the person who is doing it." – Chinese Proverb

TAKE ACTION!

think
POSITIVE

"AIM FOR THE STARS TO KEEP YOUR DREAMS ALIVE"

DATE:____/____/____

"Let your dreams be as big
as your desire to succeed"

think
POSITIVE

"When you feel you are defeated, just remember,
you have the power to move on,
it is all in your mind"

DATE:____/____/____

think
POSITIVE

"OPPORTUNITY COMES TO THOSE WHO NEVER GIVE UP"

DATE:____/____/____

"You are the creator of your own opportunities"

believe you can

"ALWAYS AIM FOR BIGGER GOALS, THEY HAVE
THE POWER TO KEEP YOU MOTIVATED"

DATE:___/___/___

"Every achievement starts with
a dream and a goal in mind"

BELIEVE IN
YOURSELF

"SUCCESS IS NOT A PLACE OR A DESTINATION,
IT IS A WAY OF THINKING WHILE ALWAYS
HAVING A NEW GOAL IN MIND"

DATE:___/___/___

"Fall seven times and stand up eight." –
Japanese Proverb

"CHANGE THE WORLD ONE DREAM AT A TIME,
BELIEVE IN YOUR DREAMS"

DATE:____/____/____

"Dreams make things happen; nothing is impossible as long as you believe."

never give up

think
POSITIVE

"Never loose confidence in your dreams,
there will be obstacles and defeats, but you will
always win if you persist"

DATE:____/____/____

"Never wait for someone else to
validate your existence, you are the
creator of your own destiny"

DATE:____/____/____

believe
you
can

think
POSITIVE

"Everything you dream is possible
as long as you believe in yourself"

BELIEVE IN YOURSELF

"A SUCCESSFUL PERSON IS SOMEONE THAT UNDERSTANDS
TEMPORARY DEFEAT AS A LEARNING PROCESS, NEVER GIVE UP!"

DATE:____/____/____

TAKE ACTION!

"MOTIVATION COMES FROM WORKING ON OUR DREAMS AND
FROM TAKING ACTION TO ACHIEVE OUR GOALS"

DATE:____/____/____

"Dreams are the foundation to our imagination and success"

think
POSITIVE

"your mission in life should be to thrive
and not merely survive"

DATE:___/___/___

"The right time to start something new is now"

think
POSITIVE

"DOING WHAT YOU BELIEVE IN, AND GOING AFTER YOUR DREAMS WILL ONLY RESULT IN SUCCESS." - ANONYMOUS

DATE:___/___/___

"Be brave, fight for what you believe
in and make your dreams a reality."

*believe
you
Can*

"The will to win, the desire to succeed, the urge to reach your full potential... these are the keys that will unlock the door to personal excellence." – Confucius

DATE:___/___/___

BELIEVE IN YOURSELF

"LET YOUR DREAMS BE BIGGER THAN YOUR FEARS AND YOUR ACTIONS
LOUDER THAN YOUR WORDS." - ANONYMOUS

DATE:___/___/___

TAKE ACTION!

think
POSITIVE

"START EVERY DAY WITH A GOAL IN MIND AND
MAKE IT HAPPEN WITH YOUR ACTIONS"

DATE:____/____/____

"If you have big dreams you will always
have big reasons to wake up every day"

DATE:___/___/___

"To achieve our dreams we must first overcome our fear of failure"

MAKE IT HAPPEN

think POSITIVE

"Difficulties are nothing more than opportunities in disguise, keep on trying and you will succeed"

DATE:____/____/____

believe you can

"Use failure as a motivation tool not as a sign of defeat"

DATE:___/___/___

"Always have a powerful reason to wake up
every new morning, set goals and follow your dreams"

DATE:_____/_____/_____

BELIEVE IN
YOURSELF

"Have faith in the future but
above all in yourself"

think
POSITIVE

"NEVER LET YOUR DREAMS DIE FOR FEAR OF FAILURE.
DEFEAT IS JUST TEMPORARY: YOUR DREAMS ARE YOUR POWER"

DATE:___/___/___

"The secret of getting ahead is getting started." – Mark Twain

"A FAILURE IS A LESSON, NOT A LOSS. IT IS A TEMPORARY
AND SOMETIMES NECESSARY DETOUR, NOT A DEAD END"

DATE:____/____/____

never give up

think
POSITIVE

"Never let your doubt blind your goals, for your future lies in your ability, not your failure" — Anonymous

"Don't go into something to test the
waters, go into things to make waves"
— Anonymous

MAKE IT HAPPEN

"Laughter is the shock absorber that softens and minimizes the bumps of life" — Anonymous

DATE:____/____/____

DATE:___/___/___

"HOPE IS A WAKING DREAM" - ARISTOTLE

DATE:___/___/___

BELIEVE IN
YOURSELF

think
POSITIVE

"NEVER GIVE UP ON A DREAM JUST BECAUSE OF THE TIME IT WILL TAKE
TO ACCOMPLISH IT. THE TIME WILL PASS ANYWAY."
– ANONYMOUS

DATE:___/___/___

TAKE ACTION!

"IF YOU WANT TO FEEL RICH, JUST COUNT ALL THE THINGS
YOU HAVE THAT MONEY CAN'T BUY" — ANONYMOUS

DATE:____/____/____

"Some pursue success and
happiness – Others create it"
— Anonymous

DATE:____/____/____

MAKE IT
HAPPEN

"IT'S BETTER TO HAVE AN IMPOSSIBLE DREAM THAN
NO DREAM AT ALL" – ANONYMOUS

DATE:___/___/___

"All things are possible if you believe"

believe
you
can

"The winner always has a plan; The loser always
has an excuse" — Anonymous

DATE:___/___/___

BELIEVE IN YOURSELF

think
POSITIVE

"There is no elevator to success.
you have to take the stairs"
— Anonymous

DATE:___/___/___

"Never let defeat have the last word" — Anonymous

DATE:___/___/___

"DON'T LET YESTERDAY'S DISAPPOINTMENTS, OVERSHADOW
TOMORROW'S ACHIEVEMENTS" — ANONYMOUS

DATE:___/___/___

think
POSITIVE

"WE ARE LIMITED, NOT BY OUR ABILITIES, BUT BY OUR VISION"
— ANONYMOUS

DATE:___/___/___

"The mind is everything. What you think you become." – Buddha

think
POSITIVE

"A JOURNEY OF A THOUSAND MILES MUST BEGIN
WITH A SINGLE STEP." – LAO TZU

DATE:___/___/___

believe you Can

"A diamond is a chunk of coal that
made good under pressure"
— Anonymous

DATE:____/____/____

"You risk more when you don't
take any risks"

think
POSITIVE

"REMEMBER YESTERDAY, DREAM OF TOMORROW, BUT
LIVE FOR TODAY" — ANONYMOUS

DATE:___/___/___

TAKE ACTION!

"Dream is not what you see in sleep, dream is the thing
which does not let you sleep" — Anonymous

DATE:___/___/___

think
POSITIVE

"DON'T BE PUSHED BY YOUR PROBLEMS.
BE LED BY YOUR DREAMS" — ANONYMOUS

DATE:___/___/___

MAKE IT
HAPPEN

"ONCE YOU HAVE A DREAM PUT ALL YOUR HEART
AND SOUL TO ACHIEVE IT"

DATE:___/___/___

"Follow your heart and your dreams will come true" – Anonymous

believe you can

DATE:___/___/___

"YOU CREATE YOUR LIFE BY FOLLOWING
YOUR DREAMS WITH DECISIVE ACTIONS"

DATE:___/___/___

"Without dreams you lose interest in life; you have no energy to move forward"

think
POSITIVE

"The road to success is always full of surprises
and temporary failures, real success comes
to those who persist and enjoy the journey"

DATE:___/___/___

TAKE ACTION!

DATE:___/___/___

"TO live a creative life, we must lose
our fear of being wrong"
- Anonymous

DATE:____/____/____

DATE: ___/___/___

"MAKE EACH DAY COUNT, YOU WILL NEVER
HAVE THIS DAY AGAIN"

"It's not what you look at that matters, it's what you see" - Anonymous

MAKE IT HAPPEN

DATE:____/____/____

"SUCCESSFUL PEOPLE MAKE A HABIT OF DOING WHAT
UNSUCCESSFUL PEOPLE DON'T WANT TO DO"
— ANONYMOUS

DATE:___/___/___

think
POSITIVE

Be Strong! It might be stormy
now, but it can't rain forever!"
- Anonymous

DATE:___/___/___

"Keep taking chances - make life a
beautiful experience and never give up"

BELIEVE IN YOURSELF

CREATIVE JOURNALS FACTORY

WE HOPE YOU LIKED YOUR JOURNAL - NOTEBOOK
PLEASE WRITE YOUR REVIEW, IT MEANS A LOT TO US!

DESIGNED BY:

SUNSHINE JOURNALS STUDIO FOR:

CREATIVE JOURNALS FACTORY

THANK YOU!

Made in the USA
Coppell, TX
18 December 2019